"In an engaging introduction to worship, Sandra Van Opstal outlines a contextual and robust theology of worship that suggests worship is more than merely singing songs—it must become a lifestyle celebration. Squarely anchored in Scripture and grounded in the character of God who compels worship, Sandra takes her reader on an inspiring yet practical journey of love—one that leads us to God's heart, one that breaks in a world of injustice but finds a healing balm through the worship of the larger Christian community."

Christopher L. Heuertz, author of *Unexpected Gifts*

"*The Mission of Worship* po . . . . ship to vital aspects of mission, challenging us to engage more deeply with issues like reconciliation, justice, suffering and the discipline of lament. Emerging from the gritty realities of Sandra Van Opstal's multiethnic urban ministry, this book explores how we can more deeply know God through the worship styles of other cultures. As an ethnodoxologist, I found myself exclaiming 'Yes!' and grabbing my highlighter. It energized and inspired me for my own work at the intersection of mission and worship."

Robin Harris, Ph.D., president of the International Council of Ethnodoxologists (ICE) and coordinator of the M.A. in World Arts at GIAL in Dallas

"Thank you, Sandra, for this powerful introduction to mission and worship. This book will broaden and deepen our worship in its forms and cultures and aspirations. It is a mighty tool that God can use to take us all—as worshipers and worship leaders alike—where we need to go. These are the God-ordained places of inclusion and hospitality, justice and reconciliation in our worship, of the 'two feet' of worship and mission that God desires for us all. Please read this book carefully and prayerfully. You will be moved, just as I have been."

Steve Roy, assistant professor of pastoral theology, Trinity Evangelical Divinity School

URBANA ONWARD

The Mission of Worship

SANDRA VAN OPSTAL

**Series editors:
Nikki A. Toyama-Szeto and Tom Lin**

IVP Books

An imprint of InterVarsity Press
Downers Grove, Illinois

InterVarsity Press
P.O. Box 1400, Downers Grove, IL 60515-1426
World Wide Web: www.ivpress.com
E-mail: email@ivpress.com

InterVarsity Press® is the book-publishing division of InterVarsity Christian Fellowship/USA®, a
movement of students and faculty active on campus at hundreds of universities, colleges and schools
of nursing in the United States of America, and a member movement of the International Fellowship of
Evangelical Students. For information about local and regional activities, write Public Relations Dept.,
InterVarsity Christian Fellowship/USA, 6400 Schroeder Rd., P.O. Box 7895, Madison, WI 53707-7895, or
visit the IVCF website at <www.intervarsity.org>.

All Scripture quotations, unless otherwise indicated, are taken from the Holy Bible, Today's New
International Version®, NIV® Copyright © 1973, 1978, 1984, 2011 by Biblica, Inc.™ Used by permission.
All rights reserved worldwide.

While all stories in this book are true, some names and identifying information in this book have been
changed to protect the privacy of the individuals involved.

Cover design: Cindy Kiple
Images: abstract background: © Matthew Hertel/iStockphoto
      hand: © Matthew Hertel/iStockphoto

ISBN 978-0-8308-3462-4
Printed in the United States of America ∞

Library of Congress Cataloging-in-Publication Data has been requested.

| P | 21 | 20 | 19 | 18 | 17 | 16 | 15 | 14 | 13 | 12 | 11 | 10 | 9 | 8 | 7 | 6 | 5 | 4 | 3 | 2 | 1 |
| Y | 30 | 29 | 28 | 27 | 26 | 25 | 24 | 23 | 22 | 21 | 20 | 19 | 18 | 17 | 16 | 15 | 14 | 13 | 12 |

Contents

I love my city! It is a delight for me to host people; I've even considered being a professional tour guide. When I prepare for people to visit Chicago, I ask them what they enjoy doing. I want to know if they are fans of sports, museums, shopping or entertainment. Knowing what they want allows me to craft a tour that will fit their desires. I love taking people to places they *want* to go.

As a Chicago native, I also know that there are places that they *need* to go. There are foods they must eat and sights they must see to fully experience our great city! There is a restaurant in my neighborhood that invented a plantain and steak sandwich called a Jibarito.[1] Whenever friends come back to visit, they beg me to take them again. While Chicago pizza is an "I *want it*," the Jibarito is an "I *didn't know I needed it*." A good guide takes you to places you want to go, but a great guide takes you places you need to go—even if they are not on Lonely Planet's top ten.

Worship leaders take people where they *want* to go. We help them enter into God's presence and encounter God in ways that are familiar and comforting. In addition, we take them to places they *need* to go to understand God more deeply. We guide them into a fuller experience of God's character, which is a difficult task that takes both theological and experiential wisdom. The problem with our worship, though, is that it doesn't often take that second step. It could be that the leader hasn't experienced the "need to go" realms of worship him- or herself, or the fellowship is resistant to anything that's not familiar.

At Urbana, InterVarsity Christian Fellowship's triennial mission conference, thousands of students from different countries worship in multiple styles and languages. Imagine twenty thousand people from various nations, languages and ethnicities in worship exalting the name of Jesus. It's an awesome sight to see a multiethnic group of emerging leaders proclaiming their love for Jesus in various expressions. Throughout the week they expand their worship vocabulary in ways that exalt God.

Participating in this multiethnic community singing and dancing is an incredible experience. A gathering like this reminds us of Revelation 7:9-10:

> After this I looked, and there before me was a great multitude that no one could count, from every nation, tribe, people and language, standing before the throne and before the Lamb. They were wearing white robes and were holding palm branches in their hands. And they cried out in a loud voice:
>
> "Salvation belongs to our God,
> who sits on the throne,
> and to the Lamb."

The vision at the end of Scripture shows us that the worship of God is a multilingual, multinational, multiethnic celebration of God's glory. Urbana is like seeing this vision in live action!

As the director of worship for Urbana, I am very intentional with the worship experience; I take people not only where they want to go, but where they need to go. This is done by choosing a diverse team, learning various styles of music and trying to offer the gifts of the global church. These students have likely had many experiences where they are worshiping with people just like them and in ways that are familiar. Why not give them a glimpse of heaven on earth?

Worship at Urbana is a foretaste of the kingdom of God in all of its diversity. The experience communicates prophetically about what worship can look like today in our churches. Urbana is no ordinary church service. Those who have been to Urbana have only one way to describe the experience: "It's just like heaven!"

As a worship leader and urban missionary, I desire to help people understand *how worship and mission intersect*. Worship is a response to God, the only one who is worthy to receive glory, and mission is the call for us to invite others to that same response. The apostle Paul says it well in Romans 12:1: "Therefore, I urge you, brothers and sisters, in view of God's mercy, to offer your bodies as a living sacrifice, holy and pleasing to God—this is your true and proper worship." Congregational worship helps us encounter this missional God and live in response to who he is and what he's about. We need our hearts and minds aligned with Jesus Christ and his mission to live lives of sacrifice and service. Looking up to God and acknowledging him for who he is becomes a catalyst for mission.

Through this book, I hope to help us as worshipers move from being consumeristic observers of God to engaged participants with God. I want us to understand where we need to go and provide some explanation of why we need to go there. We must have expression that *results* in mission. *First*, we'll look at how the mission of worship begins with experiencing the fullness of God as we engage in different forms of worship and learn from different cultural traditions. *Second*, we'll explore the mission of worship as embracing God's mission of proclaiming and demonstrating his kingdom of reconciliation and justice.

PURPOSE 1: EXPERIENCING GOD

Worship often begins by taking people where they want to go. We all want to experience God in ways that are familiar. Our way of relating, whether to God or people, develops naturally out of our personalities, experiences and cultural preferences. This preferred way of relating with God affects how we approach congregational worship. For example, some folks enjoy worshiping through reflection, while others through celebration. It is important for our felt needs to be met in worship so that we can connect with God in ways that are relevant to us as individuals. This also allows us to have an authentic experience with God in the context of our community. We are speaking a language that is fluent and makes sense to us.

A few years ago I introduced a Kenyan worship song for a missions Sunday at my church. Although the congregation seemed to enjoy the new form of worship, I could see them nervously smiling as they danced. After a few minutes in Kiswahili, I transitioned into a well-known contemporary worship song. With eyes closed, feet planted and hands lifted high, the congregation came alive at a new level. I knew I had them when their arms hit the sky! This expression was clearly more natural to them. When effortless adoration and praise springs up, it is because it comes naturally to us.

While it is natural to desire an experience of God that "fits" us, we can sometimes be egocentric or community-centric instead of God-centric. Just because something is natural to us does not mean it is good. Our natural tendencies can also be affected by the Fall. We are created to worship, but in our fallenness, our worship is often ethnocentric and self-centered. We can become worship consumers looking for worship the way that we look for the latest smartphone or electronic device. When it comes to the modern consumer of worship, comfort is king!

We live in a culture in which people want a customized tour that takes them only where they feel like going. This is easy to do in the American context, where there are so many choices. I am sure we can all recall conversations when we have either heard or said, "I was not feeling worship at that church." About this consumer approach to worship Pam Howell of Willow Creek Community Church writes:

> Can you imagine the Israelites, freshly delivered from slavery, before a mountain that trembles violently with the presence of God (Exod. 19), muttering: "We're leaving because we're not singing the songs we like. Like that tambourine song, how come they don't do that tambourine song anymore?"

"I don't like it when Moses leads worship; Aaron's better."

"This is too formal—all that smoke and mystery. I like casual worship."

"It was okay, except for Miriam's dance—too wild, not enough reverence. And I don't like the tambourine."[2]

This scene seems absurd, given that these ex-slaves had been liberated by God himself. God's people were not evaluating worship; instead they were filled with awe, fear and hope. However, many of us today come with our list of preferences and a self-centered attitude toward worship. We want certain songs, experiences or even leaders to give us what we like. That might be why we follow worship artists around—to relive an experience.

Even the songs we sing are more focused on us than on Christ himself. A quick survey of the most popular songs used in worship services shows that our focus is usually less about God himself and more about how we are responding to God. Do a quick search of your own iTunes worship songs and see how much the pronoun *I* shows up.

Pastor Mark Labberton calls this type of unbiblical, self-seeking worship "illegitimate worship." In his book *The Dangerous Act of Worship*, he talks at length about how worship reorders our reality. Skye Jethani summarizes what Labberton said at a pastors conference:

"Worship reorders reality to help us see what is true," he said. It should reorder our priorities and help us see the world differently. But quite often worship is simply a baptized version of our culture. In our worship we simply mirror what is all around us— worship of self. . . . "Fear of God is what matters most," says Labberton. "The failure of our people to live this way is a failure of our worship." The solution is not making our worship louder, faster, or more spectacular as many are in the habit of doing. Rather, we need to reevaluate what our worship is forming within our people.[3]

As worshipers, we are comfortable with the expressions, themes and forms of worship familiar to us. And that's great. People want and need spaces to experience God authentically. As created beings we want to meet God in real ways, to experience repentance, healing, freedom, restoration and joy. Each of us comes with our own issues from the week and need to come just as we are. This type of space in worship is needed. But if our worship is just about staying in our familiar, comfortable experiences, we will get stuck.

If we truly hope to go deeper in our worship with God, we may need to exchange where we want to go for where we *need* to go.

Questions for Reflection

1. What felt needs are addressed in our practice of worship? How is that reflective of our experiences and culture?

2. What themes are represented? What themes are absent?

3. How do our congregations pursue comfort and familiarity in worship?

WORSHIP IN MANY FORMS

The worship we enjoy is affected by multiple factors: our theology, denomination, social location, ethnicity and culture. Some of us really enjoy traditional liturgies and structure in worship because we appreciate that it connects us to the community of believers from the past as well churches across the globe from our same tradition. We sing songs, recite prayers and practice forms of worship that have retained traditions for hundreds of years. We enjoy the space allowed for silence and reflection.

For others, freedom is central to our worship experience, and we feel bogged down by structure. Songs are just a launching point for "real" worship, and our prayers come spontaneously by the prompting of the Holy Spirit. We enjoy the space created when loud voices shout out simultaneously in praise or weeping.

Whatever our tradition, each community has an emphasis in both *content* and *style*, leaving us with blind spots. The need is for someone who will take us where we need to go, not just where we want to go.

One major blind spot that is integral to mission is the inclusion of lament in worship. After many years of hosting young adults in urban and global short-term projects, I noticed that many of them did not have the ability to cope with the tension between the extreme poverty and injustice they saw on their trips and God's abundant goodness. The dissonance created was due to their social location as upper-middle-class college students; they had not developed a theology of suffering. The discipline of lament was absent due to the combination of church tradition and social location.

I could tell students were really struggling, so I began to host a night of prayer and invite them to enter into a time of lament. Before I lead them, I always asked them the same question: How many of you have grown up in a church experience where the discipline of lament is practiced? To this day, I have had only a few students raise their hand.

Coming from Western traditions, our discomfort with pain and emphasis on the cognitive does not encourage us to experience grief for the things that break God's heart. We would much rather meditate on the attributes of God and praise him for who he is than to enter into the pain of a world longing for the final revelation of his glory. This becomes apparent when you search for songs and prayers that help us to stand in solidarity with the poor or invite worshipers to feel the things God feels for the marginalized. A worship pastor friend and I discovered that even though there are hundreds of contemporary Christian songs, we could think of less than ten songs that lead people in lament. Expanding our practice of worship to include both praise and lament will serve us as we participate in God's mission and are exposed to the suffering of the world. When we lament, our hearts are stirred for mission: we are reminded of the need for God's grace and power in the world.

In order to experience the fullness of God, we need to encounter God in celebration and reflection, lament and joy. The psalms that were offered in Israel's worship and maintained in Christian worship throughout the centuries include both praise (Psalm 33; 116) and lament (Psalm 13; 73). Psalms of lament utilize a recurring movement from deep lamentation to celebration. Today, in most Western communities of worship the inclusion of lament is almost absent because we'd much rather avoid suffering and are in favor of celebration. Some of us have not experienced things that would lead us to developing a deep theology of suffering, which then affects our worship. Old Testament scholar Dennis Magary argues that lamentation, and the psalms of lament in particular, is important and helps us to "gripe like a Christian." He goes on to say,

> In the psalms of lament when God's people were in trouble they called out and complained to God. There is an importance to lament, but we don't talk about it in Western culture. When something bad happens we don't know what to do. [In contrast] when disasters occur across the world you will see people lamenting in the streets in a public display of lamentation. We don't do that because it has been stifled; instead we complain about God to one another.[4]

Psalms of praise are the ones we typically use in congregational worship. While psalms of descriptive and declarative praise allow us to celebrate who God is and what he has done, lament allows us to long for what he can and will do. Both praise and lament fill us up with a deep sense of hope in who God is, what he has done and what we are expecting him to do. This allows us to stand in the mess of missions, when there seems to be no hope in sight, and cry out for God to come. This deepens our faith and reliance on God's Word in mission and gives us something to celebrate. Pastor Shane Hipps says,

> Authenticity and integrity in worship means expressing both lament and praise. Each element completes the other. Without

lament, praise is little more than shallow sentimentality and a denial of life's struggles and sin. Without praise, lament is a denial of hope and grace, both of which are central to our life of faith and to God's promises. These opportunities for lament and praise are not simply about meeting personal needs. They are missional practices of authenticity, hospitality, and pastoral care.[5]

When we join together to both celebrate and lament, we communicate to one another that we are willing to "weep with those who weep" and "rejoice with those who rejoice." We enter into deeper worship expressions when we incorporate disciplines that expose us to the variety of human experiences.

While lament and celebration are only two of many expressions, the same can be said for the contrast between contemplative reflection and exuberant praise, as well as repentance and declaration of victory. We must not allow our default modes to blind us from relating to God in various ways. We must be willing to explore places we need to go in worship so we can fully experience God.

WORSHIP AND CULTURE

One year when my campus fellowship really began to experiment with diverse worship, a frustrated student, Jessica, burst out in a meeting, "Why are we focusing so much on diverse worship? . . . Why can't we *just* worship?"

After the meeting I asked Jessica what she meant by "*just* worship."

She said, "Normal worship. You know, like regular worship."

That conversation launched her into a three-year journey that would lead her to becoming the worship leader for our fellowship (and later a church) and ultimately the one answering that same question. I am continually asked, "Is singing Latino or Gospel songs really necessary if there are so few minorities in our church?" or "What value is there in singing songs if the people are not represented in our church?"

To most people it seems like a waste of time to work so hard at learning multiple styles and approaches to worship if everyone in your congregation would be happy with the way it is. The assumption made by Jessica, and many of us, is that *our* worship is "normal." What we fail to realize is that worship is contextual and therefore grounded in culture. To be sure, there are aspects of our worship that are transcultural, but much of it—the theme of the lyrics we sing, the musical style, the type of instruments we use, the way the worship leader leads—is based on our personal and collective preferences.

Culture shapes worship. Worship expression is inextricably linked with one's own culture. This includes values and norms given to us through our denominational and ethnic heritage. Most of us don't recognize our own cultural preferences, and thus have trouble realizing what we are missing from a broader perspective. We always eat pizza, so we don't know to eat Jibaritos. For example, European American culture is more linear and cognitive, which shows up in our love for teaching theology through hymns, or singing while standing still. African culture on the other hand is more affective and holistic, involving the mind, emotions and body. When we have a reference for our own cultural norms, we can be genuinely open to new expressions of worship. We need to know where we are coming from before we can enter into forms of worship that are culturally relevant to others. Displacement from our worship community by participating crossculturally helps us uncover our "normal."

There are two primary reasons that we engage in other cultural forms of worship, even if we come from a homogeneous church. The first reason is that we experience a fuller picture of God. The variety and range of God's creativity is seen and expressed in the vast artistic range of human approaches to worship. Our music, our instruments, our words, our songs and our liturgies display incredibly different facets of God's character.

As North Americans we can be enriched by the worship practices of Christians around the world. In his book *God's Global Mosaic*, Paul-Gordon Chandler gives a global glimpse of the peoples of the world through God's eyes.

The church worldwide is an extremely diverse collection of people from every country, ethnic group and culture.... The foundation for our unity as Christians throughout the world is not our likeness but our diversity.... There is one Christian faith, but many cultures. The gospel is one, but it finds expression in a variety of cultural forms as each individual's culture shapes both his or her response to Christ in understanding the gospel. Consequently Christians around the world worship God in a variety of ways.[6]

Each culture focuses on an attribute of God's character that comes out of the lived experience of that community. Various themes of spirituality are magnified through our particular ethnic lenses. Here are some of Chandler's specific observations on how cultural perspectives highlight particular aspects of God's identity or experiences with God:

- Latin American worship is about celebrating life no matter what the circumstances. It is a lively worship that brings them to trust God in the present as a community. They identify with Scriptures like Ecclesiastes that call us to laughter and joy alongside crying and grief.

- For African Christians there is a strong sense of God's power to bring freedom. The gospel is one of freedom that releases us to worship with victory.

- East Asian Christians exalt a God who is bigger than we can imagine. Worship, therefore, is about unboxing God so we can see him in his glory.

- Eastern European worship reveals a majestic and holy God.

- South Asians see God as a teacher who models and walks with us.

- For Middle Eastern Christians a life of worship is about perseverance and running the race (Hebrews 12:2).

Even if our church or fellowship itself is not diverse, multiethnic worship will expand our view of God. Too often we are waiting for our community to become more diverse before seeking a more diverse experience. We perceive that our worship is as deep or rich as it could be without an understanding of our deficiency. We see diversity as nice but not necessary. Learning to worship in diverse ways is necessary to help us encounter a God who is bigger than any one tradition or culture can express. Chandler argues that diverse forms of worship give us windows into God's majesty.

> Christianity worldwide is a *divine mosaic*, with each piece being a different cultural expression of the Christian Faith and the whole portraying the beauty of God's character as perhaps nothing else can. It is a continual learning from these many cultural expressions of Christianity that our own faith can be made most complete.[7]

One morning at Urbana 09, we decided to highlight European American traditions of worship. One of our worship team members, Andrew, who was raised in this tradition, led us through the experience. After the session an African American woman with tears in her eyes came to Andrew and thanked him for leading, saying, "I never really understood or was able to worship to hymns and liturgy. Today, I finally got it!" Diverse worship is not just about white Americans "getting it"; it's about all of us being willing to receive gifts from one another as a way of encountering God and being changed.

The second reason we engage in other cultural forms of worship is that it leads us to personal transformation. Our understanding of the church is transformed. As we worship crossculturally, we better understand our own worship as just a piece of a larger community. As we experience our differences we can more fully enjoy what it means to connect to the global church. Then we realize that we are a part of a bigger family. This helps connect us to the hearts of our brothers and sisters who live radically different lives than we live.

My husband, Karl, spent time in a primarily African American church in a lower-income community. While there he noticed that many of the songs sung during worship had themes of God's provision or the ability to overcome obstacles. He realized that his worship language, the songs he was used to singing at previous churches or devotionals, lacked these themes. Upon further reflection he realized that it made sense—his experience was a life of relative comfort and ease that didn't include the need for provision or the ability to overcome adversity. But it made sense for this community, and as he participated his understanding of God was deepened.

As a Latina who grew up in a majority white church, I was always aware that my personal expression of faith was distinct from the people who I worshiped with on Sunday. Intuitively, I assimilated to the worship style of my Southern Baptist, hymn-singing community. I enjoyed the richness of the harmonies and the beauty in the order, but I knew it didn't speak to the fullness of what worship could be. I continued on a journey through many different traditions: Vineyard, African American COGIC (Church of God in Christ), suburban megachurch and ultimately landing in a multiethnic church. At the time I was the team leader for the InterVarsity Fellowship at Northwestern University, and my work was with a black gospel choir, a Latino Bible study and a multiethnic fellowship. This fellowship had a similar demographic to the multiethnic church I had joined, which had a significant number of Asian Americans.

In the almost ten years I was at the church and on campus, I mentored a worship leader every year, all of whom were Asian American. I was changed deeply by my students and leaders at church who came from Asian American backgrounds. They taught me about what devotion and surrender looked like in worship. During this time they introduced me to CCM (Contemporary Christian Music) and in particular a song called "Blessed Be Your Name."[8] The song speaks clearly about how we are to bless God through every circumstance, knowing that he is the one who both gives and takes away. It is a picture of extreme devotion from the life of Job, who had lost everything. Job says, "Naked I came from my mother's womb, and naked I will depart. The Lord gave and the Lord has taken away; may the name of the Lord be praised" (Job 1:21). This song and the experience with Asian American students gave me words for a very difficult season as a worshiper.

I've had the honor of worshiping with and being led by African Americans, young urban professionals, white suburbanites, Asian Americans and the elderly at First Baptist of Wheeling. These experiences allow me to value the gifts I have been given by each tradition and share them across cultures. I can take the beauty of liturgy to Latino urban youth. I can take the simplicity of the less-is-more worship of Asian American devotion to bless African Americans. I can take the celebration of Latinos to white congregations that want to celebrate but need to be given permission to bust out! As a worship leader one of my goals is to share the gifts of the global church that have been passed on to me so that we can come to a fuller understanding of God and be transformed in the process.

Questions for Reflection

1. How has worshiping with people from different backgrounds changed your understanding of God?

2. What do you think could be missing from your worship?

3. How has exposure to other cultures of worship transformed you personally (more than just your thinking)?

PURPOSE 2: EMBRACING GOD'S MISSION

Worship not only allows us to experience God in all his fullness, it also creates a space for us to *hear the call to the mission of God*. As we hear Scripture and sing songs that declare his character, we are reminded that Jesus' mission extends beyond us. We are reminded that worship is not just about where we want to go, but where we need to go. In worship God meets us where we're at, and takes us further to places we have not been.

We respond to God in adoration and we're moved to worship beyond song to worship in action! Jesus is establishing his reign, and he comes proclaiming and demonstrating good news to the poor.

> The Spirit of the Lord is on me,
> because he has anointed me
> to proclaim good news to the poor. He has sent me
>> to proclaim freedom for the prisoners and recovery of sight for
>> the blind,
>> to set the oppressed free,
>> to proclaim the year of the Lord's favor. (Luke 4:18-19, arranged
>> for emphasis)

Let's take a closer look at Jesus' mission in Luke 4:18-30.

Jesus reveals his identity as Savior and his mission to proclaim and demonstrate freedom. Jesus declares his identity in the first two "me" statements of the passage. "The spirit of the Lord is upon *me*, because he has anointed *me*." The first statement reveals his identity as a prophet. Prophets of the Old Testament spoke when the spirit came upon them, and Jesus quotes this particular passage to demonstrate this. The imagery used here was to show the people that he was God's messenger. Furthermore, this is a quote from the prophet Isaiah in which God declares desire for his people to live justly (Isaiah 58; 61). In the second "me" statement he reveals his identity as Messiah (King) since the practice of anointing had messianic connotations. Jesus is not only the messenger of salvation, he is the bringer of salvation. Jesus declares his identity as prophet and Messiah—the Savior. In the last "me" statement, Jesus declares his mission: "To preach good news to the poor, he has sent *me*."

Jesus communicated that the Lord anointed him to care for the poor and the oppressed, but who exactly are the poor Jesus is talking about? First, they were the Israelites, Jesus' primary audience. This was great news to a people living in an occupied territory, on the margin, in desperate need of savior. The poor were also the economically destitute, which would often (as it does today) intersect with gender, ethnicity and vocation. Throughout the Gospel of Luke, the most comprehensive definition of the poor are the "outsiders" or those who are excluded for eco-

nomic, social, political and religious reasons. Jesus pursues those rele-
gated to positions outside the boundaries. We cannot deny that Jesus has
the spiritually poor or "pious poor" in mind as well when we take into account the Beatitudes in Matthew 5. It is to all these poor that the good
news is preached.

Just how did Jesus go about his overarching mission of proclaiming
good news to the poor in Luke? The emphasis in his activity is in the active
verbs: *proclaim*, *set free* and again *proclaim*. First, proclaiming the good
news to the poor involves exactly that: the verbal *proclamation* of
freedom. Jesus came to *proclaim* spiritual and physical freedom to those
who are imprisoned. With his words and invitations, Jesus proclaimed
that the kingdom of God is here. Our proclamation is as important as our
embodied worship.

Second, proclaiming the good news to the poor involves the *demonstration* of freedom. Jesus came to set the oppressed free. Jesus modeled
in all four Gospels a life of setting people free from spiritual and physical
bondage and oppression. This is shown in Luke as both physical healing
(Luke 7; 18; Acts 9) and salvation (Luke 1; 3). In the book of Isaiah, God is
making a complaint against Israel for not living out its calling and failing
to be a source of liberty for those who are oppressed. Jesus did what they
failed to do. He will bring salvation and an end to suffering. Now, Jesus
also invites us to do something. We are to demonstrate freedom because
our *demonstration* validates our *proclamation*.

Last, Jesus declares a new era! The context of both Isaiah 58 and 61
develops Jubilee themes, describing the coming rescue of God's people
from exile and captivity. The year of the Lord's favor, Jubilee, initiated a
new start. This context underscores the inauguration of the time of salvation and the Messiah who is to mediate God's deliverance. What does
this tell us about God? In a world where the wealthy and powerful push to
the front, God takes notice of the needs of the impoverished and vulnerable! Jesus offers salvation and new beginnings to all. He proclaims a
new start through his offer of divine deliverance. Jesus both proclaims it

and accomplishes it. The fulfillment of that which Jesus speaks must be rooted in his person. He is the messenger and the bringer of the new era!

Jesus reveals his identity as Savior and his mission to proclaim and demonstrate freedom. Worship as a congregation allows us to proclaim that a new time has begun. When we sing, we are proclaiming to God, one another and the world that there is a new King. It prepares us to receive Jesus' invitation to join him in making things new as we demonstrate freedom. This means true worship should be both a proclamation of the good news as well as demonstration.

Imagine if your community set times aside to hear testimonies of how God is at work in the world and in your city. You could invite people to share, pray for different communities and sing songs with themes about God's heart for the world. You might intentionally choose songs that are meant to be sung in community to one another as encouragement and ask that we not close our eyes as many are accustomed to doing. Imagine an opportunity to practice what Paul says in Colossians 3:16-17:

> Let the message of Christ dwell among you richly as you teach and admonish one another with all wisdom through psalms, hymns, and songs from the Spirit, singing to God with gratitude in your hearts. And whatever you do, whether in word or deed, do it all in the name of the Lord Jesus, giving thanks to God the Father through him.

The mission of worship is therefore experiencing God in all of his fullness as well as embracing God's mission to proclaim and demonstrate his kingdom of reconciliation and justice.

WORSHIP AND RECONCILIATION

My husband works internationally and often has coworkers from far away places visit Chicago. Before they arrive he makes sure that they will enjoy the different aspects of American culture, but also tries to ensure there is something familiar. For his English coworkers the morning cup of coffee is quite foreign, so he'll bring in English tea. When his associates visit from Mexico, he'll make sure that hot sauce is readily available to complement food designed for a less spicy palate. He'll also plan fun evening activities in downtown Chicago, but ensure that some evenings are low key to allow them to rest and adjust to a new culture or time zone.

This kind of hospitality is needed in our worship to proclaim and demonstrate the reconciliation of the gospel. Our worship should create an environment where God's people are welcomed. If you are a community that is committed to creating an environment that is inclusive of people from other ethnic backgrounds, consider how your worship experience reflects that.

We see this great act of hospitality in the Scriptures as the Holy Spirit is poured out on the early church. Luke's account of Pentecost shows us God's way of reaching out to humanity. Acts 2:1-8, 11-13 paints a vivid picture:

> When the day of Pentecost came, they were all together in one place. Suddenly a sound like the blowing of a violent wind came from heaven and filled the whole house where they were sitting. They saw what seemed to be tongues of fire that separated and came to rest on each of them. All of them were filled with the Holy Spirit and began to speak in other tongues as the Spirit enabled them.
>
> Now there were staying in Jerusalem God-fearing Jews from every nation under heaven. When they heard this sound, a crowd came together in bewilderment, because each one heard their own language being spoken. Utterly amazed, they asked: "Aren't all these who are speaking Galileans? Then how is it that each of us hears them in our native language. . . . We hear them declaring the wonders of God in our own tongues!" Amazed and perplexed, they asked one another, "What does this mean?"
>
> Some, however, made fun of them and said, "They have had too much wine."

In Jerusalem, where the story takes place, there were Jewish people from three different cultural groups. First, there were Jews from Judea who spoke Aramaic and felt at home in Jerusalem. Second, there were Jews from all around the region who spoke different languages, but were likely bilingual and bicultural. These also could connect. Third, there were converts to Judaism who were not ethnically Jewish and likely spoke other languages as their native tongue. (These three categories are found in many of our multiethnic churches today.) At Pentecost God honors their linguistic diversity. After the Spirit comes with power the people are enabled to speak the gospel in ways that connect with those who were present. Can you imagine? God equipped the early church with the gift of tongues so that the people would hear the gospel in their own heart language. God did not give the gift of ears, but the church was empowered to speak in someone else's cultural language. God gives them an experience that helps them feel at home and shapes the ministry of the early church with a multiethnic flavor.

All of us in some way can relate to this experience of feeling welcomed. I am sure we've each had an experience where we have gone somewhere and instinctively felt "this is home." An experience where we see or hear something that reminds us of home, and we feel included and welcomed. It happens to me when I see a colorful place, smell cilantro and onions or when someone calls me Sandrita!

There are also times when we do not feel welcomed. When people enter into communities where their heart language is not being spoken, they often feel unwelcomed. The Jews at Pentecost were there to worship at the festival time with other Jews from all over the land, and many of them probably did not feel at home in Jerusalem. But in the midst of it, God speaks to them in their own heart language. He does not ask them to check their cultural distinctiveness and the beauty of the way he created them at the door. God was letting them know he *loved* them, valued them and created them. He allows them to have an experience of hospitality where they could say to themselves, "They speak my language here!" God through the display of the Holy Spirit was creating a new community of worshipers.

In his foreword to Manny Ortiz's *One New People*, Harvie Conn says,

> Into a world where class, power, ancestry divided rich from poor, free from slave, men from women, came a revolutionary society that welcomed all who bore the name of Jesus (1 Cor 26-29). Into an ethnic oriented world that isolated Jew from Greek, barbarian from Roman, came a new kind of gathering place (Gal 3:28).[9]

The model of the New Testament church reflects a multiethnic church beginning at Pentecost and reflecting the eventual oneness we see in Revelation.

Worship is often the first thing that people encounter in our communities. Through our worship we have the opportunity to make people feel like they are right at home with love, warmth and hospitality. But by only representing one culture of worship, we may inadvertently give potential newcomers from other traditions the cold shoulder. Would you rather be mistaken as a cold congregation or a drunk congregation?

I have a white friend who attended an African American–dominant church that was seeking to be multiethnic. When asked by the leadership of the church what could make the church more hospitable to nonblack folks, he expressed a desire for more variety in the worship. He was told that they would not "water down" their worship for anyone. There seemed to be a correlation in their minds between their own cultural expression and strong worship. He eventually found a church that was more willing to embrace his expression as a legitimate form of worship.

On the other hand, one Sunday morning a young Latina woman thanked me for leading a few songs in Spanish. With tears in her eyes, Clara said, "I was about to stop coming here. This was going to be my last week at church, but when I heard you sing 'No hay nadie como tú,' it spoke to my heart so deeply. I realized this can be home for me." Clara and her husband not only continued to come to church but eventually gave significant leadership in the church community. She just wanted someone to welcome her.

The communities in which I lead worship have committed to being on a journey. They desire to invite people to be themselves. Empowered by the Holy Spirit, they celebrate the diverse design of our creative God. They enjoy and learn from one another in their uniqueness. They are saying through their worship, "We value who God has made you ethnically, and we want to invite you to be at home. We speak your language, or at least we try."

Greg, an Asian American student worship leader, said about his experience on our worship team,

> Three years ago, if you would've told me that I would be up in front of people dancing, shouting and leading black gospel, I would've called you crazy. But here I am with such different people striving to understand and approach differences, and not only tolerate them, but to really accept and celebrate them. This picture is a piece of God's kingdom, breaking into this world, saying that the gospel *really is the good news!* That God is still God, that Jesus is still good and the Holy Spirit is still alive and *very well.* Through and within these people, there has been healing, heartache and rejoicing.

Worship can be a tool for welcome! People often ask me why they should sing songs from different cultural traditions if those cultures are not represented in their church. I ask them if, when those people do show up, they would like their worship to say, "You are welcome here." This journey for me has been long. It has had its ups and downs. But there has been no greater delight than seeing a white congregation being led by an Asian American worship leader singing urban gospel!

There are great benefits in learning from those who are different from us. Congregational worship forces us to share in an experience of worship that connects us. In worship we have the opportunity to stand in solidarity with others; this brings us face to face with people who have radically different life experiences. Whether in song, hearing of testimonies or preaching, we come into communion through the experience of the other.

The focus is not an intellectual assent but an intimate encounter in community that leads us to reconciliation with humanity and better understanding of God. Miguel De La Torre writes, "Reading the Bible from the margins of society is not an exercise that reveals interesting perspectives on how other cultures read and interpret biblical texts. To read the Bible from the margins is to grasp God in the midst of struggle and oppression."[10]

A friend of ours chose to attend a church where he was a minority. Chad came from an upper-class white suburban background, and the church was predominantly Puerto Rican urban working poor. One day in service the pastor was preaching on the life of Joseph. As he talked about struggles, injustice and oppression that Joseph encountered, the congregation "Amen-ed." As Chad watched the congregation get increasingly animated and encouraged, he realized that he did not understand their encouragement because he had very little opposition in life. The experience of congregating in that community, as well as living there, transformed his perspective and made him more aware of how and why people experience poverty. Singing and serving alongside his church community actually surfaced his own prejudices and preferences. He was able to acknowledge barriers that were there for him; without this experience he may have been clueless! Through worship, Chad was able to practice reconciliation toward a community of Latinos, and the barriers began to fall.

Worship can be a place where people are still marginalized on our campuses and in our churches. The assumptions and prejudices that plague our society are alive and well in the church. We breathe the same toxins that the rest of the world breathes every time we watch the news or listen to people in our community. But imagine if the church was different, if the people who were often overlooked or distrusted were welcomed in the church through worship. What might it look like for them to be celebrated for the gifts they bring in following Jesus? Can you see it? If not, take a minute to imagine.

One day in prayer I felt led by the Spirit to include an Arabic worship song at Urbana 09 as a prophetic move toward inclusion. My friend

Miriam had taught me the song; it is sung by the Zabaleen (garbage collectors) in the beautiful slums of Mokattam, Egypt. Many people from the starting regions of the early church have felt unwelcomed by the church in North America. Some Americans experience discomfort when they see Arabic characters and hear Arabic being spoken. While some of that may be because of a general discomfort with the foreign, some is due to stereotypes and assumptions.

At Urbana 09 I looked at the participants as they danced and sang, "Ana farhan bahtef magdan lik, magdan lik, magdan lik," which in Arabic means, "I sing joyfully, glory to you God, glory to you, glory to you." It was so powerful to hear North American young people singing in Arabic and receiving the gifts of the church in the Middle East. It was powerful precisely because of the antiterrorist rhetoric that had marginalized many Middle Eastern people.

When I heard the stadium roaring in Arabic, I imagined that one day heaven would be just like that moment! Heaven will not merely be a display of people singing in different languages but a display of the divided wall of hostility being broken in its fullness (Ephesians 2:14-17).

Questions for Reflection

1. What makes you feel welcomed in worship?

2. Are you shaping your community's worship around who is presently there or a vision of what you would like to see?

3. What are you doing as a community to take people not only where they want to go but where they need to go?

WORSHIP AND JUSTICE

Worship without mission is not worship. Living a life committed to justice for all people was *the* way to live, according to my family. Growing up with family in both Argentina and Colombia, I developed an awareness of the poverty and injustice in the world. As Catholics, social action was taught as a key worship activity of Christians. We learned that our love and worship, anchored in Matthew 22:37-40, was intertwined with a call to love our neighbor:

> "Love the Lord your God with all your heart and with all your soul and with all your mind." This is the first and greatest commandment. And the second is like it: "Love your neighbor as yourself." All the Law and the Prophets hang on these two commandments.

Along with the greatest command from the lips of Jesus, my Catholic foundations highlighted the Sermon on the Mount as a lens for worship. The life and words of Jesus painted a compelling picture; in addition, the words of the prophets, such as Amos, also insisted that social righteousness is central to a life that is pleasing to God. Through his words he attacked the abuse of power and condemned Israel's worship.[11]

When we study the Old Testament prophets, we hear their strong words about worship without justice:

> I hate, I despise your religious festivals;
>   your assemblies are a stench to me.
> Even though you bring me burnt offerings and grain offerings,
>   I will not accept them.
> Though you bring choice fellowship offerings,
>   I will have no regard for them.
> Away with the noise of your songs!
>   I will not listen to the music of your harps.
> But let justice roll on like a river,
>   righteousness like a never-failing stream! (Amos 5:21-24)

Like a prosecuting attorney, Amos was charging them with their failure to live a life of true worship. While Amos is clearly addressing their idolatry, which is mentioned two times, he is highlighting their injustice and abuse of the poor by mentioning it five times. He charges them with the following:

- becoming self–important
- using wealth as a means of luxury
- neglecting the poor
- treating people like commodities
- perverting justice in the courts
- idolatry

Like other prophets, such as Isaiah and Micah, he described the abuse and evil of society and appealed to God's people to repent of these sins.[12] He doesn't give them an out either, making clear that indirect oppression is no more acceptable than direct oppression; it is still sin against God himself. Continuing to worship through rituals when not living justly only adds to transgression. Amos 5 clearly argues that *true worship cannot exist without justice.*

The sharp language used in this passage conveys the revulsion of God. The Lord is saying to these "worshipers," "I can't stand your worship, I can't stomach the stench." The Israelites were sitting in their own filth and probably had no idea how bad they smelled. It's like being on a road trip for more than twelve hours and getting used to your odor. You do not even realize how bad you smell! The Lord goes on to say through Amos, "I will not look at you." Their worship had become a mechanical means of appeasing their God. They had pretty buildings, pretty objects, pretty songs, but they were not beautiful to the Lord because they lacked justice. There is a clear movement in the text that encompasses all the senses: from smelling to seeing to hearing. At this point the Lord just says, "Shut it! Away with your singing." Their soulless worship was a burden to the Lord and he was fully disgusted. How might the Lord experience our worship today? We gather in pretty buildings with pretty music and neglect the vulnerable people we drive or walk past on our way there. We produce "Christian" products without ever asking about the work conditions of those who manufactured them.

True worship is not about style or form! True worship has little to do with music or offerings or services—but with seeking God and living in response. We need to be cautious and hear this clear warning from Amos. The ethics of a worshiper matter; our lives must overflow with righteousness and justice. Our religious lives are *busy*—and we can think we're cool because of all our activities, but true worship requires mercy and justice toward others and obedience to God's commands. Mark Labberton writes,

> *Worship* names what matters most: The way human beings are created to reflect God's glory by embodying God's character in lives that seek righteousness and do justice. Worship turns out to be the dangerous act of waking up to God in the world, and then living lives that actually show it. . . .
>
> True worship includes the glory and honor due to God—Father, Son and Spirit. It also includes the enactment of God's love and justice, mercy and kindness in this world.[13]

When was the last time you heard a sermon from Amos or any other prophet as a part of the "worship wars" discussion at church?[14] We may need to repent that our focus has been on the style of worship versus the content of our worship, which includes God's teaching about justice. How might the Lord experience us today if he smelled, saw and heard our "worship"? Compare how much time and money we have spent consuming "Christian" worship CDs, concert tickets and books to the attention we have given in caring for the needs of the poor. He might say to us:

I hate, I despise your weddings,
   and I take no delight in your prayer meetings and worship services.
Even though you offer me your tithes and spring-break service
      projects,
   I will not accept them.
And the clothing donations of your full closets

I will not look upon.
Take away from me the noise of your Hillsong and Kirk Franklin;
to the melody of your guitars, mandolins and keyboards I will
not listen.
But let justice roll down like waters,
and righteousness like an ever-flowing stream.[15]

This warning is especially concerning given the "worship concert" phenomenon where we spend hundreds of dollars in ticket fees, parking and purchases to "worship" alongside thousands of other people. I'm saying this as a woman who regularly leads worship at events with thousands of people present. But if such large gatherings lead us to an "intimate" experience of God but never to mission, I question why we do them. We must ask where our larger worship movements are going. Are they leading us to experience God in fuller ways and embrace his mission of reconciliation and justice, or are they only leading us to an experience that we've had before but with better musicians and a larger crowd?

I hope for something much more than that when I am planning for worship at Urbana. I am trying to create a space where people from all different ethnic backgrounds can come together and experience God more deeply in order to be mobilized for global mission. I am hoping that the worship in songs becomes worship with hands and feet. I am praying that students will seek God and embody lives of mercy and justice. My prayer is that we will cultivate worship through our finances by giving to ministries that will advance the mission of God. That we will cultivate worship with our time by serving the marginalized. That we will cultivate worship with our influence as a global citizen in advocating in issues such as education, sex trafficking and immigration.

Questions for Reflection

1. The things the Israelites were doing were offensive to God—they courted his wrath. How do we do the same thing? List the activities

that we personally participate in that make us busy in "worship." How can those things distract you from true worship?

2. What are the things that we allow to shape our understanding of God and worship?

3. What does worship in our churches look like? How does that practice shape our theology?

4. What are the ways that injustice works in our society? Where is there corruption?

5. What are ways that we deprive the poor of justice?

6. What do righteousness and justice look, smell and sound like? How can we make it flow? Who have you seen who did this?

Mission without worship is not God's mission. For over fifteen years I have been mobilizing students to mission through weekly evangelism and service, global short-term projects and urban programs. In my last position as the Chicago Urban Program director I connected students to churches that were living out their worship in the context of the city. In this program, college students live in an intentional Christian community in which they examine issues of justice, poverty, racism, racial identity and reconciliation in the context of service and evangelism.

One trend I see is students prone to activism growing in volunteerism while not growing in their worship of God. Students are active in doing good deeds but often disconnected from biblical understanding and communion with God. They are focused on the mission of justice but distant from the God who defines what is just. While I am not quite ready to jump on the beware-of-social-justice bandwagon, I want to warn those who want to do God's work without seeking God. In Amos 4, the call to the Israelites was to seek God and repent (or turn to him). Our worship of God requires that we find our starting place for mission in God himself. The sad story is that many of us who are activists often get lost in the mission activity and not in the Lord. We place one "religious activity"—churchgoing, Bible memorization, worship services—with other "religious activity"—homeless ministry, mission trips and political activism.

That summer, while living in Mokattam, the Egyptian village of garbage collectors outside of Cairo, I came to grips with my activism. It was hard to worship because I often felt overwhelmed by the amount of work, the depth of injustice and poverty, or the passivity of the Western church. I found it easier to play with the orphans, teach lessons to the boys at the recycling center or clean people's homes. Worship and prayer were difficult, and I felt very disconnected from God. I remember one night as the smell of the village overcame me and the sound of the Muslim prayers shouted at me, I threw my hands in the air and cried, "Where are you, God?"

Feeling overwhelmed by the whole experience drew me to a deeper encounter with God, but I had to call out to him, not ignore him or run from him. I threw myself on the rough rooftop and asked God what he wanted me to do. His answer was not "fix it" or "work harder." His answer was "seek me." In the context of what felt like a very short mission trip, God led me to a time of fasting, ceasing and prayer that helped me see God present in the people and the mission he had called me to.

Our mission must be filled with worship—responding to God in adoration and praise. We must acknowledge his presence in the mission. The people of God practiced the sabbath in order to remember the works of God in liberating them. They reenacted God's rest as a way to celebrate who God was and what he had done. Nicholas Wolterstorff says that for Christians the center of worship is remembrance of Christ's resurrection and anticipation of his coming kingdom.[16] He urges us to consider practicing a rhythm of work and worship (rest) to celebrate God's work. Our worship allows us to center our works in the context of our remembrance and abiding in God. Therefore worship is critical to the context of our works of justice. Worship and works need to authenticate one another. Wolterstorff writes,

If worship is performed and works of justice and mercy are missing, then a shadow is cast over worship, and its authenticity questioned. For this same God whom we are to worship by celebrating his deeds in memorial also requires of us that, in grateful response to those deeds, we take heed of him by doing the works of mercy and justice. But can we not also say that if the works of mercy and justice are performed but their worship is missing, then a shadow is cast over those works, and their authenticity is brought into question. For that very same God, whom we are to heed by doing the works of mercy and justice in gratitude for those deeds of his that we re-member and expect, also requires of us that we celebrate in me-morial those deeds: *work and worship are mutually authenticating.*[17]

In other words, mission without worship is just as off-center as worship without mission. When we worship and rest, we remind ourselves that we are not the Holy Spirit but are in partnership with God. When we worship we see God for who he is and anticipate the day when he, not we, will make all things new. In communion with God, we see accurately that God is en-gaged in a world that is both his and ours, but a world in which he is Lord and we are not.[18] When asked what makes our works of justice distinctive to that of a social service agency, I say, "Our worship." The mission comes from God, but the work itself is done in partnership with God as well.

Worship reminds us that God is present and he is good. We are re-minded in worship that the power to overcome evil and effect change comes from Christ himself. Worship expert Robert Webber says,

What happens in worship is that our struggles with the powers of evil that disturb us and seek to dismantle our relationships and our lives are brought to Jesus the victor over all evil. In worship we deal again and again with the ultimate truth that Jesus, who overcame the powers of evil through his death and resurrection, is able to overcome those powers of evil that are now at work in our own lives.[19]

As an urban missionary, and someone who is committed to my neighborhood and its need for God's shalom, I can often pursue works of justice on my own. I work long hours, overextend myself and view rest as something that weak people need. Over the past five years I have been working with my neighborhood association on affordable housing. Because of the rise in rental prices in our community, many families were being split up or displaced, and housing was scarce. Over the years I have attended community meetings, spoken with our city council representative, collected signatures and spoken at city hall. Every time we thought the project would go through, we encountered a new barrier. The only reason I survived this five-year project for affordable housing was because of the worship of the members of the community.

In this predominantly Latino and African American community, Christian faith and worship played an integral role in the experience. Our experience involves an understanding of God as the bringer of freedom and provision. God has set us free in the past and we know he will do it again. Latinos have an ability to celebrate God in the midst of suffering and hardship that surpasses one's circumstance.[20] Being in community with these Latino and African American believers encouraged me to enter into worship (and rest) not because I was weak or optimistic but because I could be confident in God's power as I was reminded of what he had already done. The rhythms of worship and work made the long haul to the end sustainable. When I walk by the construction sites of the housing on my way home from Zumba, I celebrate God and the worship he accomplished. Work and worship do authenticate one another.

On the sabbath we remember what happened before and look with hope to what is to come. At the center is the resurrection of Christ. That is the grand story of which we take part! If we take that reflection out of our worship, what is the reason for our work? If we do not worship, we lose the significance of our work, and that's because worship allows us to remember and anticipate the work of God past, present and future.

One day, as I awoke early, I heard God invite me to worship. It was a call to slow down, fast and pray. For four days in the hot Egyptian sun I did just that, and I experienced a centeredness, an attentiveness to God's presence and a joy that I had not experienced before. Worship and work of justice and mercy go hand in hand.

WORSHIP CAN MOBILIZE PEOPLE FOR MISSION

Worship can be an instrument of transformation and catalyst for works of justice. Leaders can create space to inform people of God's will and form their heart to ways of caring for the poor. An essential motivation for worship, offered by theologian Marva Dawn, is to "form believers to be disciples, following Jesus and committed to God's purposes of peace, justice and salvation in the world."[21] Richard Johnson of Spark Ventures confirms this in his study on churches that do justice. He writes,

> Churches need communal worship that is conversion-oriented: worship that weekly renews and realigns hearts and minds to the integral mission of the Christian faith they profess. That is what is happening in the communal worship of the churches in this study. Through a justice-infused liturgy and the opportunity for transformational, intimate encounters with God, these churches have created a weekly conversion-oriented worship experience for their congregations.

Our worship communities need songs that speak of God's heart for the lost and marginalized. We need prayers that allow us to stand in solidarity with the prayers of our brothers and sisters around the world. We need to hear Scripture that develops in us a prophetic imagination that addresses the structural and systemic issues of injustice.[22] We need to confess our own complicity with injustice. When I hope to help people enter into God's compassion for the poor, I try to link people with the stories and experiences of the poor and broken by leading them in songs they know that have the same theme and words. I want to bridge them from what they know to experiences of worship that are not about themselves.

Worship thus becomes a multifaceted bridge into broader expressions of praise and deeper experiences of God's grace and unlimited faithfulness. How do we serve as both prophetic voice and interpretive guide to our congregations? Ultimately, the Holy Spirit is the author of transformation, but those of us who are worship leaders have a pastoral responsibility to lead our communities to places they have not been.

We must create immersion experiences that allow people to enter into space to embrace God's mission. These experiences are intentionally planned to provide the catalyst for change. Those planning worship must answer two vital questions:

1. What do we want people to understand (cognitive)?

2. What do we want people to feel (affective)?

Practically speaking, we should include the reading of Scripture, visual elements such as symbols and media, and storytelling or testimonies. We should also have response times that include moments for self-examination and confession. Sometimes using a structure such as Psalm 139:23-24 may help. We may invite people to write down blessings they've received or prayer concerns, while other times we simply sit in silence before the Lord.

Our worship is to be missional. It needs to take people where they want to go as well as where they need to go.

While I listened to a popular song, which paints a picture of Revelation 7:9-12, I realized that the song could be enhanced by mirroring the actual text. As I prayed about how to bring the song to Urbana, I received an image of the people of God walking into the throne room of God. This image helped us to create an arrangement of the song, which included both changes in instrumentation and a multilingual layering.[23] In the months leading up to the conference we led this song in fear and trembling because it contained four languages that were hard to learn. God surprised us by making it our most powerful pastoral moment in any venue in which we sang it. Whether an older white church in Wisconsin or a multiethnic group of students in Texas, God showed up powerfully. One evening a South Asian man approached me and thanked me for painting a beautiful picture of what worship will be like. He expressed that singing in all the languages gave him a deeper passion to hear the language of his present community. It gave him a heart for outreach on his campus, and a vision of the kingdom. Every time I have led this song, I introduce it by sharing the Scripture and image the Lord placed on my heart. It has served to be a powerful tool for mobilizing people in worship.

Questions for Worship Leaders

1. *Forms.* Consider your set list. Are all your songs celebratory? Is their room for lament? Have someone other than you describe the themes of your songs.

2. *Cultures.* Have you experienced worship in a church or fellowship where the ethnic makeup is not your own? Perhaps you can join a church or group where the worship experience is different from your own.

3. *Hospitality.* Is your worship welcoming to those different from you? Is it preparing your congregation or fellowship to be welcoming to others? Don't just sing a Spanish song—explain why it's needed.

CONCLUSION: WALKING WITH BOTH FEET

A few months ago I was leading worship for over six hundred college students and having a blast. The passion in the room was palpable, and as students erupted in celebration, I was moved by their joy. As I sang "I Am Free" I was moved from dancing to jumping. Then all of a sudden I heard a *snap* and felt the floor drop underneath me. Actually the floor had not dropped, but my Achilles tendon had snapped.

The students continued to worship as I signaled the band to keep going, and I hopped off the stage. At the hospital I had to keep repeating my story to each medical professional. I would say, "I was leading worship, and jumping, and I . . ." The whole thing seemed ridiculous. They asked, "Do you have any other injuries?" I explained that I had snapped my other Achilles ten years ago on a mission trip to China.

After retelling the story so many times, I realized the Lord has given me a physical illustration for worship and mission. Worship and mission are like two feet that are both needed to walk with the Lord.

Culturally, it seems that the default mode for engaging with worship comes from reality television. We're fans, we watch, we like, but we don't see ourselves as actively involved. We are spectators and consumers, but not engaged in worship that leads us to mission. We are hopping around on one leg.

We need both feet, unless you'd like to hop around on crutches all day. When I look down at my matching scars, I will always be reminded that worship and mission are inseparable. As worshipers we need to move from being consumeristic observers of God to engaged participants with God. We must have expression that *results* in mission. It's just as the prophet Micah says about our worship,

> With what shall I come before the Lord
>> and bow down before the exalted God?
> Shall I come before him with burnt offerings,
>> with calves a year old?
> Will the Lord be pleased with thousands of rams,
>> with ten thousand rivers of olive oil?
> Shall I offer my firstborn for my transgression,
>> the fruit of my body for the sin of my soul?
> He has shown you, O mortal, what is good.
>> And what does the Lord require of you?
> To act justly and to love mercy
>> and to walk humbly with your God. (Micah 6:6-8)

What can we possibly bring before the Lord in our worship? Just our songs? Our words? Our enthusiasm? No! The Lord requires us to enact justice, be merciful and walk in humility, asking him where we need to go instead of walking where we want to go.

What would it look like for the next generation of worshipers to move to a deeper mission of worship? What places might the Lord be taking you? Imagine communities of believers experiencing the fullness of God and embracing his mission in the world. My hope as a worship leader and urban missionary is that we would all walk humbly with our God using both feet, in worship and in mission.

APPENDIX
FURTHER RESOURCES

Songs for Crossing Cultures

Culture	Style	Artist
Latino		
Noy Hadie Como Tú (No one like you)	Slow	Marco Barrientos
Nombre No Hay (No other name)	Upbeat	Freddy Rodriguez
Eres Todo Poderoso (You are all powerful)	Rock	Rojo
Montana (Mountain)	Upbeat	Salvador
Gospel		
Say So	Upbeat	Israel Houghton
Praise the Lord with Me	Med Tempo	Bishop T. D. Jakes
I Give Myself Away	Slow	William McDowell
Freedom	Upbeat	Eddie James
CCM		
How Great Is Our God	Med Tempo	Chris Tomlin, Passion
The Stand	Med Tempo	Hillsong United
Revelation Song	Slow	Kari Jobe
How He Loves	Slow	Kim Walker-Smith, Jesus Culture
Crossover Hymns		
Great Is Thy Faithfulness		
Amazing Grace		
I Surrender All		
Oh How I Love Jesus		
Global (from Urbana 09 and 12)		
Magdan Lik (Glory to you)	Upbeat	Arabic (Egypt)
Hakuna Mungu Kama Wewe (There's no one like Jesus)	Upbeat	Kiswahili (Kenya)
Yesu Azali Awa (Jesus Christ is with us)	Med Tempo	Congolese (Congo)
Yeshu Tera Naam (Jesus your name is higher)	Med Tempo	Hindi (India)

Books

Worship

Peterson, David G. *Engaging with God: A Biblical Theology of Worship*. Downers Grove, Ill.: InterVarsity Press, 1992.

Webber, Robert E. *Worship Old and New*. Grand Rapids: Zondervan, 1994.

Diverse Worship

Maynard-Reid, Pedrito U. *Diverse Worship*. Downers Grove, Ill.: InterVarsity Press, 2000.

Yancey, George. *One Body, One Spirit*. Downers Grove, Ill.: InterVarsity Press, 2003.

Mission

Chandler, Paul-Gordon. *God's Global Mosaic*. Downers Grove, Ill.: InterVarsity Press, 2000.

Labberton, Mark. *The Dangerous Act of Worship*. Downers Grove, Ill.: InterVarsity Press, 2007.

Websites

Ancient Future Worship, www.ancientfutureworship.com

"Come to the Table" blog, https://urbana.org/blogs/come-table

Heart Sounds International, www.heart-sounds.org

Worship Matters, www.worshipmatters.com

NOTES

[1]This tasty Puerto Rican sandwich was created at Borinquen restaurant in Humboldt Park, a neighborhood on Chicago's northwest side.

[2]Pam Howell, "Can You Engage Both Heart and Mind?" *Leadership Journal*, April 1, 1999.

[3]Skye Jethani, "Worship That Reorders Reality," *Out of Ur*, February 13, 2007, www .outofur.com/archives/2007/02/post.html. These concepts are covered in detail in Mark Labberton, *The Dangerous Act of Worship* (Downers Grove, Ill.: InterVarsity Press, 2007).

[4]This comes from a lecture on poetry and psalms of the Old Testament, Dr. Dennis R. Magary, "OT Poetic and Prophetic Books," Trinity Evangelical Divinity School.

[5]Shane Hipps, "Praise That's Premature: Do We Praise Too Soon?" *Leadership Journal*, April 1, 2007.

[6]Paul-Gordon Chandler, *God's Global Mosaic* (Downers Grove, Ill.: InterVarsity Press, 1996), p. 16.

[7]Ibid., p. 17.

[8]This song was written by Matt Redman as a response to 9/11, given the fact that we as a community did not have enough songs of lament to deal with the crisis. It makes the claim that we should not practice a passive fatalism but actively praise God by acknowledging the circumstances.

[9]Harvie M. Conn, foreword in Manuel Ortiz, *One New People* (Downers Grove, Ill.: Inter-Varsity Press, 1996), p. 9.

[10]Miguel A. De La Torre, *Reading the Bible from the Margins* (Maryknoll, N.Y.: Orbis, 2002), p. 4.

[11]Richard Foster, *Stream of Living Water* (San Francisco: HarperOne, 2001).

[12]Clear calls to worship as the enactment of justice can be found in Isaiah 58 and Micah 6.

[13]Labberton, *Dangerous Act of Worship*, p. 13.

[14]"Worship wars" refer to the tension in many churches today between traditional and contemporary styles of worship.

[15]Paraphrase of Amos 5:21-24.

[16]Nicholas Wolterstorff, *Until Justice and Peace Embrace* (Grand Rapids: Eerdmans, 1983), p. 156.

[17]Ibid., p. 157.

[18]Ibid., p. 152.

[19]Robert Webber, *Worship Is a Verb: Celebrating God's Mighty Deeds of Salvation* (Peabody, Mass.: Hendrickson, 1992), p. 205.

[20]More explanation of these themes can be found in *Diverse Worship* by Pedrito Maynard.

[21]Marva Dawn, *A Royal "Waste" of Time: The Splendor of Worshiping God and Being Church for the World* (Grand Rapids: Eerdmans, 1999), p. 343.

[22]Foster, *Stream of Living Water*.

[23]This song can be found on the Urbana Student Missions Conference 2012 Worship CD.

About Urbana

Since InterVarsity Christian Fellowship/USA and Inter-Varsity Canada's first Student Missions Conference in 1946, Urbana has influenced more than 250,000 people to devote their lives to God's global mission. Urbana's mission is to compel this generation to give their whole lives for God's global mission. Participants are challenged by missions leaders, are able to speak with hundreds of missions organizations, get to attend an amazing selection of seminars and tracks, and study the Bible inductively with other students listening for God's call on their lives. For more information, visit www.urbana.org.

Urbana Onward

God calls us to go into the world as his representatives. But we need not travel alone. Urbana Onward provides companions for the lifelong journey into missional living. This series offers concise resources for grappling with challenging issues. Trusted authors provide biblical and practical insights for following God's call in creative and courageous ways. Discover a bigger picture of God's global mission as he leads you onward.

Pursuing God's Call by Tom Lin, 978-0-8308-3459-4

Partnering with the Global Church by Nikki A. Toyama-Szeto and Femi B. Adeleye, 978-0-8308-3460-0

The Mission of Worship by Sandra Van Opstal, 978-0-8308-3462-4

Your Mind's Mission by Greg Jao, 978-0-8308-3461-7

Deepening the Soul for Justice by Bethany H. Hoang, 978-0-8308-3463-1

Spiritual Warfare in Mission by Mary Anne and Jack Voelkel, 978-0-8308-3464-8